BATAVIA PUBLIC LIBRARY DISTRICT

3 6173 00153 3085

W9-BDB-696

Officially Noted

Blue writing
4/24/07

"Neither we, nor any other people, will ever be respected till we respect ourselves and we will never respect ourselves till we have the means to live respectfully."

— FREDERICK DOUGLASS

CORBIS/Bettmann

FREDERICK DOUGLASS

BY JOHN PASSARO

The Child's World®

BATAVIA LIBRARY
BATAVIA, ILLINOIS 60510

GRAPHIC DESIGN
Robert E. Bonaker / Graphic Design & Consulting Co.

PROJECT COORDINATOR
James R. Rothaus / James R. Rothaus & Associates

EDITORIAL DIRECTION
Elizabeth Sirimarco Budd

COVER PHOTO
Portrait of Frederick Douglass by CORBIS

Text copyright © 2000 by The Child's World®, Inc.
All rights reserved. No part of this book may be reproduced
or utilized in any form or by any means without written
permission from the publisher.
Printed in the United States of America.

Library of Congress Cataloging-in-Publication Data
Passaro, John, 1953-
Frederick Douglass / by John Passaro.
p. cm.
Summary: Examines the life and accomplishments of
Frederick Douglass, as well as his impact on
the civil rights movement.
ISBN 1-56766-621-3 (library : reinforced : alk. paper)

1. Douglass, Frederick, 1817?-1895 — Juvenile literature.
2. Abolitionists — United States — Biography — Juvenile
literature. 3. Afro-American abolitionists — Biography —
Juvenile literature. 4. Slaves — United States — Biography —
Juvenile literature.
[1. Douglass, Frederick, 1817?-1895. 2. Abolitionists. 3. Afro-
Americans — Biography] I. Title

E449.D75P37 1999
973.8'092 — dc21   99-19252
[B]   CIP

Contents

Growing Up in Slavery   6

Escape from Slavery   14

An Abolitionist   21

A Nation at War   25

The Fight for Civil Rights   30

Timeline   36

Glossary   37

Index   39

Growing Up in Slavery

Frederick Douglass was born in the *slave state* of Maryland. He was probably born in February 1817 or 1818, but he never knew his birthday. At the time, few *slaves* in the southern United States knew exactly how old they were. Frederick's mother, Harriet, was a slave. This meant that Frederick was a slave, too.

Harriet worked long hours in the cornfields. She had little time to take care of a baby. Harriet's *master* was a man named Captain Aaron Anthony. He decided that baby Frederick would be better off living with his grandmother. Grandmother Betty lived on the same *plantation,* but she was still 12 miles away.

Harriet saw Frederick only a few times after that. She could only visit him at night, after she finished her work. She had to travel the 12 miles on foot and return by sunrise. When Frederick was about seven years old, Harriet died. No one told him until many years later.

As a young child, Frederick spent most of his time playing near his grandmother's cabin. He loved his grandmother. He admired the way she walked with her shoulders straight and her head held high. One day, she told Frederick they were taking a trip. She took him to the biggest, most beautiful house on the plantation. It was the home of Captain Anthony. Betty told him the slave children playing in the yard were also Harriet's children. They were his brother and his two sisters.

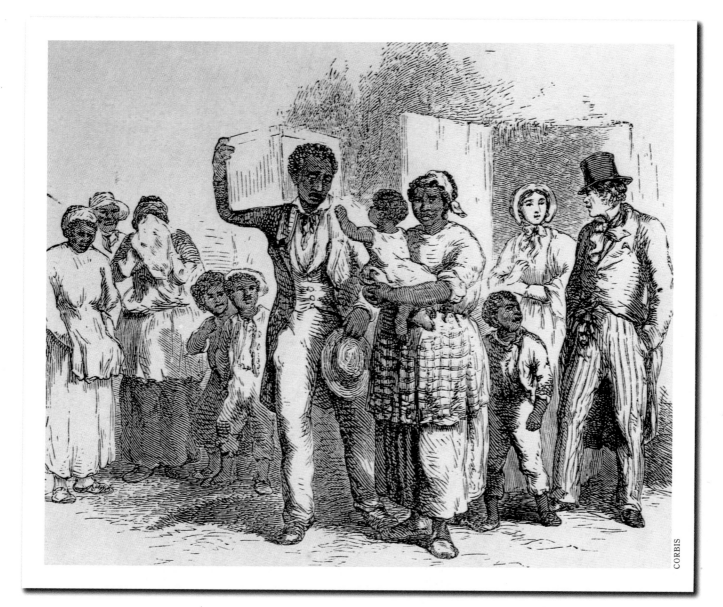

CORBIS

One terrible thing about slavery was that family members often were separated from each other. Harriet's master took her son Frederick away. He wanted her to spend all her time working in the fields.

CORBIS/Bojan Brecelj

SLAVERY WAS PERMITTED IN AMERICA FOR MORE THAN **200** YEARS. THE SLAVES CAME FROM THE AFRICAN CONTINENT. AFRICAN PEOPLE WERE KIDNAPPED BY SLAVE TRADERS AND THEN SENT TO AMERICA IN CHAINS.

Frederick was afraid to leave Betty's side. He refused to play with the other children, but she told him he must. Suddenly, Frederick's grandmother was gone. The children told him the master had sent her to another farm and that Frederick could no longer live with her. Frederick threw himself on the ground and cried. It was at this moment that he first realized he was a slave. For the first time, he knew exactly what that meant.

For many days, Frederick wondered why he had been born a slave. Why was he different from white people? Most masters did not treat their slaves well. They bought and sold them like land, tools, animals, or any other piece of property. It was as though they were not even human beings.

Captain Anthony was a cruel master. The slaves often called him "Old Master" when he wasn't around. He gave all the slave children only one shirt to wear. They had no other clothing of any kind. They did not even have shoes! Most of the time, Captain Anthony fed his slaves ground-up corn. He poured it in wooden troughs, like those used to feed pigs or cows. There was so little food, the children had to fight one another to get enough. Sometimes, they used broken seashells to scrape up the last bits of corn from the trough. At night, the children had no beds in which to sleep nor blankets to keep them warm. They slept on the cold, damp floor of the kitchen, huddled together around the stove.

SOUTHERN FARMERS TRADE A BLACK SLAVE FOR A HORSE. SLAVES WERE TREATED NO DIFFERENTLY THAN LIVESTOCK.

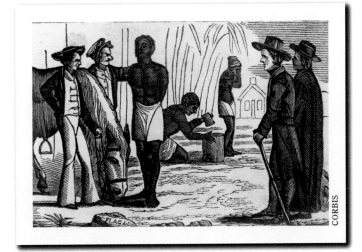

CORBIS

One night, Frederick awoke to the screams of his Aunt Hester in the next room. Through a crack in the kitchen wall, Frederick saw Captain Anthony whipping her. Frederick had never seen someone beaten so brutally. Anthony whipped Aunt Hester until his arms were too tired to go on. Blood dripped from Hester's shoulders and onto the floor. Frederick feared that the Old Master would come for him next. Captain Anthony did not beat Frederick that night, but he beat him several times in the weeks ahead.

Frederick faced starvation, cold, and beatings. Still, he grew into a bright young man. Even Captain Anthony recognized this. His daughter Lucretia gave Frederick a pleasant job. He became the playmate of the Anthony children.

One day, Frederick learned that he was going away. Captain Anthony planned to send him to the city of Baltimore. He would have a new master, a man named Hugh Auld. Mr. Auld was Lucretia's brother-in-law. Lucretia told Frederick to wash himself. She gave him a pair of pants to wear. Soon Frederick was on his way to the Auld home. The trip took three days. During the brief trip, Frederick felt free. They were the three happiest days of his young life.

Most children feel frightened and sad to leave home alone. Frederick did not. He had no reason to feel close to his home or to the people who lived there. His mother was dead. His grandmother lived far away. He seldom even saw her. He had been separated from his brother and sisters when he was very young. Now they did not even feel like family. Slavery had made them almost like strangers. "I could not feel that I was leaving anything which I could have enjoyed by staying," Frederick later remembered.

CORBIS-Bettmann

SLAVERY MEANT THAT PLANTATION OWNERS DID NOT HAVE TO PAY PEOPLE TO WORK IN THEIR FIELDS. MANY SOUTHERNERS BECAME RICH BECAUSE OF THE FREE LABOR THE SLAVES PROVIDED.

CORBIS

MASTERS OFTEN PUNISHED THEIR SLAVES WITH HARSH BEATINGS. FREDERICK HATED SLAVERY. HE KNEW IT WAS WRONG. WHEN HE GREW OLDER, FREDERICK REMEMBERED HIS DIFFICULT CHILDHOOD. "THE THOUGHT OF BEING A SLAVE FOR LIFE BEGAN TO BEAR HEAVILY UPON MY HEART," HE ONCE SAID.

In Baltimore, Mrs. Sophia Auld put Frederick to work. He ran her errands and cared for her baby. She also began to teach him to read and write. When Hugh Auld found out, he became very angry. He believed that slaves should not be taught such skills. Many slave owners felt this way. If slaves were *literate*, they could learn about the world outside the South. They might discover that there were places in the United States where slavery was illegal. An educated slave might try to escape.

Auld ended Frederick's lessons, but it was too late. Frederick realized that reading and writing might be a path to freedom. He began to study even harder. He made friends with poor white children he met while running his errands. They offered to help him study. He gave them pieces of bread in exchange. Soon he could read books and newspapers. He learned that many people thought slavery was wrong. Some people wanted to stop it.

Later, Frederick went to work for Lucretia's husband, Thomas Auld. Like Captain Anthony, Thomas was a cruel master. He starved his slaves. They had to steal food from nearby farms just to have enough to eat. Auld also beat his slaves. He and the plantation workers beat Frederick badly many times. He watched as they beat other slaves even more brutally. Frederick feared he might be a slave for the rest of his life.

Even with so many hardships, Frederick was an unusual young person. He did everything he could to improve his life. At age 15, he organized Sunday church services for other slaves. Thomas Auld did not like this. He led a mob of white people who stopped the services. They did not want the slaves to gather together. What if the slaves made plans to help one another escape at the meetings? Auld decided that Frederick was making trouble. He had to learn to obey.

Escape from Slavery

Auld sent Frederick to live with a man named Edward Covey. He was a "slave breaker"— a poor farmer who made extra money by beating disobedient slaves. In return, the slaves worked on Covey's farm. Slaves were "broken" when they became less *rebellious*. Then they were returned to their masters. Auld decided this was the only way to make Frederick obey him.

One day, a pair of oxen got away from Frederick as he worked in the fields. Covey whipped him. The leather whip cut deep scars into Frederick's back. Covey beat him nearly every day. Once he beat him so brutally that Frederick could not get up from the ground. Covey kicked him in disgust and walked away.

Then Covey decided to give Frederick the worst whipping of all. He tried to tie Frederick to a post. Suddenly, Frederick decided to fight back. He grabbed Covey by the throat. They fought for two hours. Covey finally gave up.

Covey was ashamed that a black, teenaged boy had defeated him. He sent Frederick back to Auld. Frederick had changed. He no longer feared his master. It was only a matter of time before he would escape from slavery.

The first time Frederick tried to escape, he was caught. He went to jail for one week. Thomas Auld thought Frederick had caused too much trouble. He sent him back to his brother Hugh in Baltimore.

Hugh Auld put Frederick to work in the shipyards. Each week the shipyard company paid him a small salary. He would return home and give Auld most of the money. If Frederick earned six dollars, Auld might give him six cents. Auld was the master. The money belonged to him by law. Auld hoped the pennies he gave Frederick would make him work harder. They only made him angry. Frederick worked to earn the money. He believed he had a right to keep it.

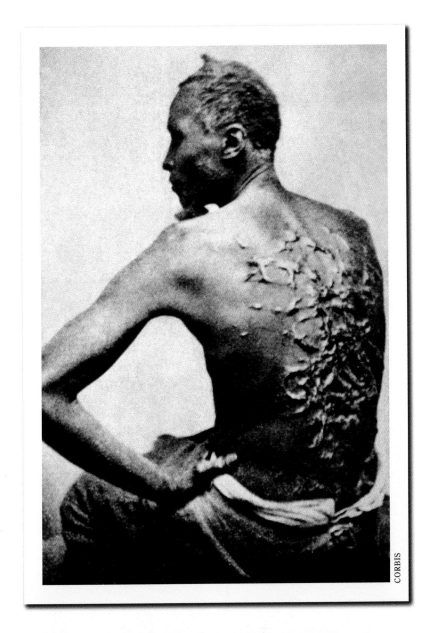

CORBIS

SOMETIMES MASTERS BEAT SLAVES SO BADLY THAT THEY HAD HORRIBLE SCARS FOR THE REST OF THEIR LIVES.

When he was not working, Frederick tried to meet other educated blacks. He joined the East Baltimore Mental Improvement Society. It was a group of educated, free *African Americans*. Most of these people had been slaves at one time. Some had managed to buy their freedom. Others were set free by their masters.

Douglass learned to *debate* at the group's meetings. He practiced his public speaking. Soon he was a skilled *orator*. He also met a free African American named Anna Murray. They fell in love and hoped to marry. He yearned for freedom more than ever.

The decision to escape slavery was difficult for Frederick. He feared he would never see Anna or his friends again if he escaped. Many runaway slaves were caught and severely punished. Slave catchers made a lot of money capturing runaways. Even so, Frederick was determined to be free. He borrowed money from Anna. He dressed up as a sailor and caught a train headed north on September 3, 1838. A few days later, he was in New York. Frederick Douglass was a free man.

Schomburg Center for Research in Black Culture

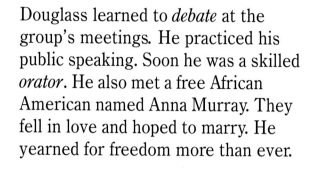

FREDERICK MET ANNA MURRAY IN BALTIMORE AT THE MENTAL IMPROVEMENT SOCIETY. HE HOPED TO MARRY HER ONE DAY.

CORBIS-Bettmann

FREDERICK KNEW IT WAS DANGEROUS TO TRY TO ESCAPE. STILL, HE COULD NOT BEAR THE THOUGHT OF A LIFETIME OF SLAVERY. IN 1838, HE MADE HIS WAY TO FREEDOM.

In New York, Douglass learned about the *Underground Railroad*. It was a secret organization that helped runaway slaves. "Conductors" on the Underground Railroad were people who helped slaves to freedom. They helped them travel to free states in the North. Sometimes, the conductors offered a safe place to stay during the day, when angry masters were looking for them. Other times, the conductors carried slaves in a wagon or boat. They always traveled at night to the next "station" on the railroad.

Soon Frederick sent for Anna Murray. They were married in New York City. Then they traveled on the Underground Railroad to New Bedford, Massachusetts. There Frederick found work in the shipyards. For the first time, he was rewarded for his labor. No one took away the money he earned. In 1839, Frederick and Anna had their first child, a daughter named Rosetta.

It was not long before Frederick learned that whites in the North did not treat blacks as equals. Employers never gave blacks the best work. They offered them only simple jobs, such as sweeping the docks and loading boxes. He faced other forms of *discrimination* as well. He could not sit with white people in church. He could not vote. He could not enter many public places. Frederick may have escaped slavery, but he still was not free.

CORBIS

TWO RUNAWAY SLAVES IN THE NORTH. ESCAPED SLAVES FACED SEVERE PUNISHMENT IF THEY WERE CAUGHT. FREDERICK WAS NOT AFRAID. HE STILL PLANNED TO MAKE HIS WAY TO FREEDOM.

This map shows some of the routes on the Underground Railroad. Frederick and Anna traveled on the secret railroad to New Bedford, Massachusetts. They hoped to start a new life together in the North.

THE LIBERATOR.

VOL. I.]   WILLIAM LLOYD GARRISON AND ISAAC KNAPP, PUBLISHERS.   **[NO. 17.**

BOSTON, MASSACHUSETTS.]   OUR COUNTRY IS THE WORLD—OUR COUNTRYMEN ARE MANKIND.   [SATURDAY, APRIL 23, 1831.

THE LIBERATOR
IS PUBLISHED WEEKLY
AT NO. 11, MERCHANTS' HALL.

WM. LLOYD GARRISON, EDITOR.

TERMS.

☞ Two Dollars per annum, payable in advance.
☞ Agents allowed every sixth copy.
☞ No subscription will be received for a shorter period than six months.
☞ All letters and communications must be POST PAID.

AGENTS.

CHARLES WHIPPLE, *Newburyport, Mass.*
JAMES E. ELLIS, *Providence, R. I.*
PHILIP A. BELL, *New-York City.*
JOSEPH CASSEY, *Philadelphia, Pa.*
HENRY OGDEN, *Newark, N. J.*
WILLIAM WATKINS, *Baltimore, Md.*

THE LIBERATOR.

'Is not the plea, that emancipation is impracticable, the most impudent hypocrisy and the most glaring absurdity ever propounded for contemplation?— Can any suppositious expediency, any dread of political disorder, or any private advantage, justify the prolongation of corruption, the enormity of which is unequalled, or repel the holy claim to its extinction? The system is so entirely corrupt, that it admits of no cure but by a TOTAL and IMMEDIATE abolition. For a gradual emancipation is a virtual recognition of the right, and establishes the rectitude of the practice. If it be just for one moment, it is hallowed for ever; and it be inequitable, not a day should it be tolerated.'

BOTANY.

two committee men and a constable interfered, and would not permit him to take his seat! He was finally driven away, and the pew passed into other hands.

We purpose shortly to visit all our meeting-houses, and ascertain what places are provided for the accommodation of our colored people. A house dedicated to the worship of Almighty God, should be the last place for the exercise of despotic principles.— But here is the extract:

'With deep regret we have observed some articles in the columns of the "Liberator," of Boston, apparently from this city, in which its inhabitants are implicated; and which we believe the editor of that publication will deem very injudicious, as well as unkind, when knowing the truth in the case. So far from wishing to deprive the colored population of an opportunity to worship God, by the co-operation of the friends of religion with that part of the inhabitants, a good and convenient house was erected a few years since; clergymen of different denominations have often officiated, gratuitously, from Sabbath to Sabbath; and when disappointed at their request, and made exertions to promote the prosperity of their congregation; for many years a Sabbath School has been taught, composed entirely of colored children and adults; in addition to this, if we mistake not, at their request the public school money is given them in proportion to the number of their children, and they thus have a day school of their own.

After such interest had been shown for that class of people, was it to be expected that an attack should be made upon the very persons who have shown such liberality? This is indeed gratifying to the enemies of benevolent exertions; and were the

be elevated and improved in this country; unanimous in opposing their instruction; unanimous in exciting the prejudices of the people against them; unanimous in apologising for the crime of slavery; unanimous in conceding the right of the planters to hold their slaves in a limited bondage; unanimous in denying the expediency of emancipation, unless the liberated slaves are sent to Liberia; unanimous in their hollow pretence for colonizing, namely, to evangelize Africa; unanimous in their *true motive* for the measure—a terror lest the blacks should rise to avenge their accumulated wrongs. It is a conspiracy to send the free people of color to Africa under a benevolent pretence, but really that the slaves may be held more securely in bondage.' It is a conspiracy based upon fear, oppression and falsehood, which draws its aliment from the prejudices of the people, which is sustained by duplicity, which is impotent in its design, which really upholds the slave system, which fascinates while it destroys, which endangers the safety and happiness of the country, which no precept of the bible can justify, which is implacable in its spirit, which should be annihilated at a blow.

These are our accusations; and if we do not substantiate them, we are willing to be covered with reproach.

In attacking the principles, and exposing the evil tendency of the Society, we wish no one to understand us as saying, that all its friends are equally guilty, or actuated by the same motives. Nor let him suppose, that we exonerate any of them from

virtue. I doubt not this conviction will ultimately prevail in every community, where the obligations of religion and philanthropy are acknowledged; though the process may be slow; having to contend with much ignorance prejudice and error. This conviction, however, is but the first step towards a result so desirable as the total abolition of slavery. Every long established custom acquires a strong hold on the feelings of those who are habituated to its control; we know that its power in many cases is almost unconquerable; and this is especially the case, where a custom, however injurious in its tendencies, is a source of pecuniary emolument, or worldly aggrandizement to those interested in its continuance. It therefore becomes necessary for the attainment of this great and good object—the universal emancipation of our colored brethren—the complete overthrow of this abominable traffic in human flesh—to investigate the whole subject fairly and calmly; to discuss it fully and freely; to ascertain, as far as possible, what are the best means and methods for the accomplishment of this great end. On this point, I find there is great diversity of opinion. Men of equal talents, equal piety, and equal benevolence, take different and almost opposite views of the whole subject: my mind has been much perplexed, by hearing what seemed to me very strong arguments on both sides of the question.

With regard to the main subject, universal emancipation, as I before remarked, I have no doubt. I think it may, and it ought to be accomplished; but with regard to the means of its accomplishment, I do not feel so decided.

CORBIS-Bettmann

DOUGLASS READ THE ANTI-SLAVERY NEWSPAPER, *THE LIBERATOR*. A WELL-KNOWN ABOLITIONIST NAMED WILLIAM LLOYD GARRISON PUBLISHED THE PAPER FOR 35 YEARS.

An Abolitionist

Many Americans believed slavery was wrong. These people became known as *abolitionists*. They wanted slavery to be abolished, or ended forever. In 1833, a group of white people formed a group called the American Anti-Slavery Society. William Lloyd Garrison was their leader. Garrison's group published books about slavery. It also published a newspaper for abolitionists called *The Liberator*.

CORBIS-Bettmann

Douglass read *The Liberator*. In August 1841, he met Garrison at a meeting. The next day, Garrison heard Douglass give a speech about his life as a slave. Douglass had a beautiful, deep voice. He used *dramatic* words to tell a story. People liked to listen to Frederick speak. Garrison asked him to give lectures for the American Anti-Slavery Society.

Douglass was an excellent speaker. Some people doubted he had ever been a slave. A few even said that he made up his stories. How could a runaway slave be so intelligent? How could he speak so well?

> ABOLITIONIST WILLIAM LLOYD GARRISON PUBLISHED *THE LIBERATOR* FOR 35 YEARS. HIS BELIEFS OFTEN MADE PEOPLE ANGRY. IN FACT, THE STATE OF GEORGIA OFFERED A $5,000 REWARD FOR HIS ARREST.

NARRATIVE

OF THE

LIFE

OF

FREDERICK DOUGLASS,

AN

AMERICAN SLAVE.

WRITTEN BY HIMSELF.

BOSTON:
PUBLISHED AT THE ANTI-SLAVERY OFFICE,
No. 25 CORNHILL
1845.

Frederick Douglass

CORBIS-Bettman

DOUGLASS' FIRST BOOK WAS PUBLISHED IN 1845. HE CONTINUED TO WRITE BOOKS ABOUT HIS EXPERIENCES IN THE YEARS THAT FOLLOWED.

Frederick wanted to prove these people wrong. He decided to write a book about his life. His friends warned him against it. Douglass was still a runaway slave. In fact, he was still the property of the Aulds. The book might help slave catchers find him. If he published his story, he risked returning to a life of slavery.

Frederick still wanted to tell his story. In the winter of 1844, he wrote *Narrative of the Life of Frederick Douglass, an American Slave*. It was published the next year. All the copies sold out in the North. It sold well in many European countries as well. The next summer, Frederick traveled to England. Many English people wanted to hear him speak.

Two English friends wanted to help Frederick. They raised enough money to buy Frederick's freedom from the Auld family. They agreed to set him free for about $700. On December 5, 1846, Hugh Auld signed the papers. Frederick Douglass was truly a free man.

THE DOUGLASS HOME IN ROCHESTER, NEW YORK.

Frederick returned to the United States after 19 months in England. He and Anna moved to Rochester, New York. He started an anti-slavery newspaper of his own called *The North Star*. African Americans wrote for the paper. While Douglass lectured and traveled, Anna raised their four children. Anna also worked in a shoe factory to help support the family. She was a steady and brave woman.

Frederick and Anna also began to help runaway slaves. Their home became a station for the Underground Railroad. Anna Douglass often fed and cared for runaways in their home. Over the years, they helped hundreds of African Americans escape to freedom.

Schomburg Center for Research in Black Culture

CORBIS

MORE THAN **600,000** SOLDIERS LOST THEIR LIVES DURING THE AMERICAN CIVIL WAR. AT FIRST, UNION SOLDIERS FOUGHT ONLY TO REUNITE THE NATION. AS YEARS PASSED, MANY PEOPLE REALIZED THAT THE WAR WAS ALSO ABOUT ENDING SLAVERY.

A Nation at War

In 1861, Americans from the South decided to form their own country. They called it the Confederate States of America. The northern states did not like this. They did not want the United States to be broken in two. The North decided to go to war against the South, and the *American Civil War* began.

The North battled the South for four long years. More than 1.5 million soldiers served in the North's Union army. More than 800,000 southerners fought for the Confederate army. By 1865, almost 620,000 men — from both the North and the South — had died fighting the war.

Frederick Douglass had become a well-known abolitionist. He asked to meet with President Abraham Lincoln, and the president agreed. Frederick asked Lincoln to end slavery. At first, the president refused. His goal was to defeat the South and reunite the nation. What would happen if he freed the slaves? Perhaps the Union would lose the support of some of its people. Lincoln decided not to take that risk.

DOUGLASS MET WITH PRESIDENT ABRAHAM LINCOLN SEVERAL TIMES DURING THE AMERICAN CIVIL WAR. THE TWO MEN CAME TO RESPECT AND ADMIRE EACH OTHER.

CORBIS-Bettmann

Eventually Lincoln changed his mind. On January 1, 1863, he signed the *Emancipation Proclamation.* This freed millions of Confederate slaves. Of course, the South refused to obey this rule. They still considered themselves to be a different country than the North.

The Union army decided to allow blacks to *enlist* in its forces. Douglass began to *recruit* African Americans to fight for the North. His own sons were among the first to enlist. More than 200,000 blacks fought in the Civil War. About 38,000 black soldiers were killed or wounded. Many black *regiments* were known for their bravery.

Despite their dedication, discrimination was still a problem for blacks in the army. Black soldiers were paid only half of what whites earned. Many white soldiers refused to serve in the same units as blacks. Whites would not allow blacks to become *officers,* either. They did not want a black man telling them what to do.

CORBIS-Bettmann

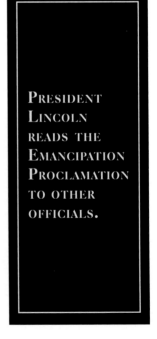

PRESIDENT LINCOLN READS THE EMANCIPATION PROCLAMATION TO OTHER OFFICIALS.

(reprocess photo)

CORBIS-Bettmann

THE 54TH MASSACHUSETTS REGIMENT, MADE UP ONLY OF BLACK TROOPS, ATTACKS FORT WAGNER IN CHARLESTON, SOUTH CAROLINA.

CORBIS-Bettmann

UNION OFFICERS REST AT THEIR CAMP AS A BLACK SERVANT WAITS ON THEM. BLACKS WERE NOT ALLOWED TO SERVE IN WHITE REGIMENTS, BUT THEY OFTEN WORKED AS SERVANTS FOR WHITE SOLDIERS AND OFFICERS.

Such poor treatment finally caused Douglass to stop recruiting African Americans for the army. He asked President Lincoln to help the black soldiers. Lincoln could not make any promises. He knew discrimination was wrong, but he also knew he could not change everything all at once.

President Lincoln's secretary of war promised to make Douglass an officer. Unfortunately, this never happened. The secretary only made the promise so that Douglass would recruit for the army again. He never truly believed whites would accept a black officer. Douglass was disappointed. Even so, he started to recruit again. Douglass knew how important it was that the North win the war.

By 1864, it looked as though the North would end the war successfully. The nation reelected President Lincoln. Officials did not invite blacks to the party at the White House, but Lincoln insisted that Douglass attend. When the president saw him come in, he said, "Here comes my friend Douglass."

UNION SOLDIERS REMOVE CHAINS FROM AN ESCAPED SLAVE AFTER PRESIDENT LINCOLN SIGNED THE EMANCIPATION PROCLAMATION INTO LAW.

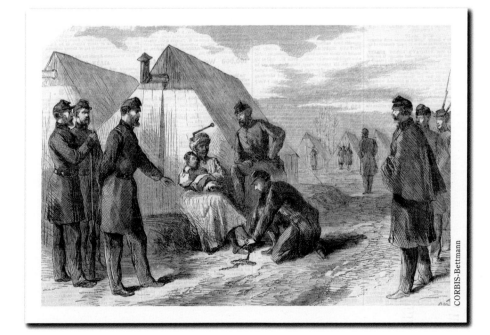

CORBIS-Bettmann

The Fight for Civil Rights

On April 9, 1865, the Civil War ended. The U.S. government reunited the nation and ended slavery. Just five days later, President Lincoln was murdered. Douglass felt he had lost a friend.

Slavery was finally illegal. Other abolitionists believed it was time to end the American Anti-Slavery Society. Douglass knew better. African Americans still faced many problems.

Employers seldom paid black workers fairly. In the South, police arrested blacks without jobs and put them in jail. Laws in the South also allowed employers to hire young black children. They paid them almost nothing. Blacks could not own property. They could not vote. They were not allowed to attend public events with whites.

Douglass knew the fight for *civil rights* had only just begun. He and other African American leaders refused to give up. Finally, a few things began to change. In 1866, Congress passed a law giving medical and educational help to southern blacks. Two years later, it passed the 14th Amendment to the Constitution. This guaranteed civil rights to African Americans. In 1870, the 15th Amendment finally gave black men the right to vote.

Women in the United States would not be able to vote until 1920. Douglass believed women were no different from men — they also deserved equal rights. In the *North Star*, he once wrote, "Right is of no sex, truth is of no color." He attended the first women's rights convention in the United States. He also supported the *suffragists,* who hoped to win the right to vote for women.

AFTER THE CIVIL WAR, MANY FORMER SLAVES HAD NOWHERE TO GO. THEY STRUGGLED TO FIND WORK. FAMILIES HAD NO HOMES AND LITTLE FOOD TO EAT. MANY WHITE PEOPLE STILL TREATED AFRICAN AMERICANS POORLY.

CORBIS

Over the years, Douglass experienced many personal difficulties. His home burned to the ground in an accidental fire. He lost his most valuable possessions. He started a new newspaper, but it failed. He became president of a bank that loaned money to African Americans. It failed as well. Most difficult of all, his wife Anna died in 1882.

Douglass also experienced many successes. He wrote two more books about his life. He held many important political positions. In 1877, the government appointed him a United States *marshal.* This was a reward for his commitment and service to his country.

Douglass once visited the Auld plantation where he had worked as a slave. He met with Thomas Auld, his former master. Auld greeted his ex-slave as "Marshal Douglass." The two men talked. They disagreed about whether slavery was right or wrong. They disagreed about the outcome of the Civil War. Finally, Auld apologized for the way he treated Douglass and the other slaves. The former slave and master were able to leave each other with less anger — and with dignity.

Schomburg Center for Research in Black Culture

DOUGLASS' WIFE ANNA DIED IN 1882. HE REMARRIED TWO YEARS LATER. HIS NEW WIFE WAS A WOMAN NAMED HELEN PITTS DOUGLASS (RIGHT).

Schomburg Center for Research in Black Culture

FREDERICK DOUGLASS IN THE DISTRICT MARSHAL'S OFFICE. DOUGLASS BECAME THE MARSHAL OF WASHINGTON, D.C., IN 1877.

Douglass continued to lead the African American fight for civil rights until he died of a heart attack on February 20, 1895. He had attended a suffragist meeting that day. To the end, Frederick Douglass never lost sight of his goals.

Black public schools across the nation closed on the day of his funeral. Thousands of people gathered to honor a true American hero. They remembered a man who courageously fought for civil rights. They remembered a man who was not afraid to speak out for what he believed. Today Douglass is remembered as the strong, firm voice of African American freedom.

CORBIS/Joseph Sohm; ChromoSohm, Inc.

FREDERICK DOUGLASS DIED IN 1895 AT THE AGE OF 77 OR 78. HE WAS BURIED NEAR HIS HOME IN ROCHESTER, NEW YORK.

CORBIS

DOUGLASS TAUGHT AMERICANS — BOTH BLACK
AND WHITE — THAT FREEDOM IS NOT ALWAYS
FREE. SOMETIMES PEOPLE MUST FIGHT FOR IT.

Timeline

1817 or 1818	Frederick Douglass is born in February. He lives on the plantation of Captain Aaron Anthony.
1826	Douglass travels to the city of Baltimore to work for Hugh Auld.
1833	Douglass works for Thomas Auld.
1834	Douglass is sent to the farm of Edward Covey, a slave breaker.
1836	Douglass attempts to escape. He fails and spends one week in jail.
1837	Douglass meets his future wife, Anna Murray.
1838	Douglass escapes to New York. He marries Anna Murray.
1841	Members of the American Anti-Slavery Society ask Douglass to speak at meeting.
1845	*Narrative of the Life of Frederick Douglass* is published. Douglass travels to England.
1847	Douglass publishes the first edition of *The North Star* newspaper.
1861	The American Civil War begins.
1863	Douglass meets with President Lincoln to discuss the mistreatment of black soldiers during the Civil War.
1865	The Civil War ends. President Lincoln is murdered.
1870	The 15th Amendment is enacted. Black men are granted the right to vote.
1874	Douglass becomes the president of the Freedman's Savings and Trust Company.
1877	Douglass becomes the U.S. Marshal of Washington, D.C.
1882	Anna Murray Douglass dies.
1884	Douglass marries Helen Pitts.
1895	Frederick Douglass dies.

Glossary

abolitionists
(ab-o-LISH-e-nests)
Abolitionists were people who wanted to end slavery in the United States. William Lloyd Garrison was a well-known abolitionist.

African Americans
(AF-ri-kan uh-MAYR-ih-kanz)
African Americans are black Americans whose ancestors came from Africa. Frederick Douglass was an African American.

American Civil War
(uh-MAYR-ih-kan SIV-el WAR)
The American Civil War was fought between the North and South. The war lasted for four years between 1861 and 1865.

civil rights
(SIV-el RYTZ)
Civil rights are the personal freedoms that belong to all citizens of the United States. The Constitution guarantees civil rights.

debate
(dee-BAYT)
When someone debates, they take one side of an issue and argue for or against it. Frederick Douglass learned to debate when he joined the East Baltimore Mental Improvement Society.

discrimination
(dis-krim-ih-NAY-shun)
Discrimination is the unfair treatment of a person simply because they are different. African Americans have suffered discrimination by whites.

dramatic
(dreh-MAT-ik)
If something is dramatic, it is striking or powerful. Frederick Douglass had a dramatic way of speaking.

Emancipation Proclamation
(ee-MAN-se-PAY-shun prok-le-MAY-shun)
The Emancipation Proclamation was a presidential act that was signed on January 1, 1863. When President Lincoln signed the Emancipation Proclamation, he freed millions of slaves.

enlist
(in-LIST)
If someone enlists, he or she joins a country's military. Frederick Douglass' sons enlisted in the Union army.

literate
(LIT-e-ret)
If a person is literate, he or she can read and write. Slave owners did not want their slaves to be literate.

marshal
(MAR-shel)
A marshal is a law officer with duties similar to those of a sheriff. Frederick Douglass was appointed as the marshal of Washington, D.C.

master
(MAS-ter)
A master is an owner of a slave. Captain Aaron Anthony was Frederick Douglass' first master.

Glossary

officers
(OFF-e-serz)
Officers are people in the military who are in charge of the troops. During the American Civil War, blacks could not be officers in the Union army.

orator
(OR-et-er)
An orator is a person who is very good at speaking to the public. Frederick Douglass was a skilled orator.

plantation
(plan-TAY-shen)
A plantation is a large farm (or several farms together) that grows crops. Before slavery was abolished in the United States, many plantations used slaves for free labor.

rebellious
(reh-BEL-yes)
If a person is rebellious, he or she disobeys authority. Rebellious slaves were severely punished.

recruit
(reh-KREWT)
If someone recruits others, he or she encourages them to join the military or other group. Frederick Douglass recruited black men to join the Union army.

regiments
(REJ-e-mentz)
Regiments are smaller groups of soldiers within an army. Many black regiments in the Union army were courageous and dedicated.

slaves
(SLAYVZ)
Slaves are people who are forced to work for others without pay. Slavery became illegal in the United States when the North won the Civil War.

slave state
(SLAYV STAYT)
A slave state was one of the American states where slavery was legal. Frederick Douglass was born in the slave state of Maryland.

suffragists
(SUFF-ruh-jists)
The suffragists were women who fought to win the right to vote in the United States. Women were finally allowed to vote in 1920.

Underground Railroad
(UN-der-grownd RAYL-rohd)
The Underground Railroad was a group of people who helped African Americans escape slavery. Frederick and Anna Douglass helped hundreds of runaway slaves escape on the Underground Railroad.

Index

abolitionists, 21, 23, 25, 30
American Anti-Slavery Society, 21, 30
American Civil War, 24-29, 30
Anthony, Aaron, 6, 9, 10, 13
Auld, Hugh, 10, 13, 14, 21-22
Auld, Lucretia, 10, 13
Auld, Sophia, 13
Auld, Thomas, 13, 14, 33

civil rights, 30, 34
Confederate States of America, 25
Constitution, amendments to, 30
Covey, Edward, 14

discrimination, 18, 26, 29
Douglass, Anna (Murray), 16, 18, 23, 32
Douglass, Frederick
  and beatings, 10, 13, 14
  children of, 18, 23, 26
  death of, 34-35
  education of, 13
  in England, 21, 23
  and escape, first attempt, 14
  and escape from slavery, 16, 17
  and grandmother (Betty), 6, 9, 10
  marriages of, 18, 33
  as marshal of Washington, D.C., 32-33
  and mother (Harriet), 6, 10
  and public speaking, 16, 21
  and purchase of from Hugh Auld, 21, 23
  siblings of, 6, 9, 10
  soldiers, recruitment of, 26, 29
  writings of, 21-22, 33
Douglass, Helen Pitts, 32

East Baltimore Mental Improvement Society, 16
Emancipation Proclamation, 26, 29

54th Massachusetts Regiment, 27

Garrison, William Lloyd, 20-21

Liberator, The, 20-21
Lincoln, Abraham, 25-26, 29
  death of, 30

Narrative of the Life of Frederick Douglass, an
  American Slave, 21-22
North Star, The, 23, 30

plantation, 6, 11

slave breaker, 14
slave state, 6
slaves,
  cruel treatment of, 9-10, 12, 13, 14, 15
  and difficulties after the Civil War, 30-31
  and escape, dangers of, 16, 18
  and literacy, 13
  separation of families, 6-7
soldiers, African American, 26-29
  discrimination against, 26, 28, 29
suffragists, 30, 34

Underground Railroad, the, 18, 19, 23
Union army, 25-26, 27, 28, 29
  and African American soldiers, 26-29

voting rights, 30

women's rights, 30

For Further Information

Books

Archer, Jules. *They Had a Dream: The Civil Rights Movement from Frederick Douglass to Marcus Garvey to Martin Luther King and Malcom X.* New York: Puffin, 1996.

Carey, Charles. *The Emancipation Proclamation (Journey to Freedom).* Chanhassen, MN: The Child's World, 1999.

Douglass, Frederick. *Escape from Slavery: The Boyhood of Frederick Douglass in His Own Words.* New York: Knopf, 1994.

Web Sites

Visit the National Park Service's exhibit on Frederick Douglass:
http://www.cr.nps.gov/csd/exhibits/douglass/

Learn more about Douglass' involvement in the American Civil War:
http://americancivilwar.com/colored/frederick_douglass.html

Visit the Frederick Douglass Museum On-Line:
http://www.ggw.org/freenet/f/fdm/index.html